Sister Sue
My Dear
I hope you enjoy this
book. JC Beichner, Jennifer,
was sharing her life at our
Church and promoting her
book — I was inspired so
here is your copy.

Merry Christmas
and Blessings in
this next — New Year.

Love John
+ Joan

GRACE
IN
PROGRESS

Prayers for the Beautifully Broken

J.C. BEICHNER

JC BEICHNER
PUBLISHING

Print ISBN: 978-1-48358-669-4

eBook ISBN: 978-1-48358-670-0

Cover art photo by Joshua Earle, www.joshuaearlephotography.com, courtesy of Unsplash. Cover design and J.C. Beichner Publishing logo by Gabe Rauch, Copyright © 2016 all-rights reserved.

The prayers titled "Glorify" and "Unfinished" were inspired by Life Teen International themes of the same name and were written and dedicated to serve the teens of Life Teen at St. Patrick Catholic Community in Scottsdale, AZ, no copyright infringement is intended.

All for Him.

"Christ in me arise and dispel all the darkness.

Christ in me arise with your power and your strength.

Christ in me pour out your blessing and healing.

Christ in me arise and I shall rise with you."

-Trevor Thomson

"The sinner that's inside of me, has lost all his control of me."

-Matt Maher

Acknowledgements

My heartfelt gratitude goes out to all of my dear family and friends who have never stopped encouraging me from listening to God's call in my heart. Every prayer, every shared moment of tears and laughter has ministered to me and helped me create this humble offering. To Kate Olmscheid, my invaluable Copy-Editor-in-Chief and also Gabe Rauch, for his creative insights and beautiful cover design, I am indebted to you both. Above all, I especially want to thank my husband, David for his patience and understanding of the late nights and wild ideas and for loving me through it all. Life is ministry and I would not choose to minister in this life with anyone else but you. I also want to thank the St. Patrick Catholic Community of Scottsdale, Arizona, where true conversion is possible and discipleship is alive and well.

Contents

Introduction

This collection of prayers was once called "Embracing His Grace." It began as a personal process to challenge myself through my faith to write more and deny my gifts less. In writing for myself I often would have amazing creative inspirations and produce great work only to become bogged down in negative inner dialogue telling me my work was self-centered and not up to par. Writing is a solitary endeavor, and I have often struggled with my worthiness to sit in the chair and allow God to work through me. I began this collection of prayers as a devotion of trust. I wanted to take action to show my intention and commitment to allow Jesus to heal the broken parts of my heart that would not let God's love in. I wanted to do something that would say, "Thank you, Lord."

This book of prayer is a battle won, a triumph in the holy struggle. It is grace in progress. Faith can be elusive at times in this world when we knock up against bad choices, persecution or tragedy. Yet Christ loves us perfectly and knows we are but a wonderful work to be completed through Him. No matter how crooked our paths may be or how far we may sometimes wander from Him, He is always there waiting, with arms wide open, ready to welcome us back home. These prayers are my story, my experience of Christ at work in my life, but also a devotion to the community that has loved and supported me through it. My hope is that through these prayers you will be encouraged to trust God more, rely on your own ways less and embrace the depth of God's love in the ordinary moments of your life. My hope is that you will find the heart within your heart, where your story of grace begins, and discover where Christ most needs to abide in your life.

Foreword ❀ My Story

M y favorite part of the mass is when we all stand and lift our hands towards the altar, towards God, and say, "Lord, I am not worthy that you should enter under my roof, but only say the word and my soul shall be healed." At first, I found this profession quite odd. Under my roof? What does that even mean?

But I came to love this part of the mass because as we are gathered together, we all stand up and profess our brokenness. Together. Right then and there we are being asked to take a personal inventory of who we have been in the past week, how we have lived, how we have treated one another and how we have treated ourselves. It is an examination of conscience, a moment of truth and self-awareness before God and our community. We are called to look within ourselves, examine our hearts and then reflect back where we most need God to abide in us. "Lord, I am not worthy that you should enter under my roof, but only say the word and my soul shall be healed." And then we go to receive Communion. Our walk towards the altar is symbolic of our journey towards Christ. We are walking to the Eucharist. In those beautiful moments we are the prodigal son and we are walking home, running back into the arms of our loving Father and all is forgiven.

Everything under my roof.

The above reference comes from scripture and can be found in Matthew 8:8 and more completely in Luke 7:1-7, which gives a detailed account of a Roman Centurion whose slave was sick. The Centurion believes Jesus can heal his slave but he doesn't believe he is worthy to ask Him to do so. I am not yet a theologian, but in short, the Centurion's friends go to Jesus on his behalf, because he is a decent man, and they ask Jesus to come to the house to heal his slave. Jesus goes to the Centurion's house but as He approaches, the Centurion stops Him and tells Him he is not worthy for Him to enter under his roof. He tells Jesus of his authority to order people around and make them do his bidding but he is powerless to heal his sick slave. He needs Jesus but does not presume to ask for himself but for his slave and Jesus rewards his faith.

What needs to be healed under our roof? Think of all that happens day in and day out under the roof of your house. What did your parents used to say when you would get into trouble? "Not under my roof! You aren't doing that under my roof!" But everything under the roof means everything that God knows and loves us for, everything that we have ever done, everything that we may do and all the ways that we fail Him. Again, everything under the roof. Not only are we not worthy to ask Him to come under our roof, but there is a lot of stuff under our roof--there's even more under the rug!

You know the biggest thing about accepting God's love for us, that love we can't even stretch our minds around, that great mystery of the perfect, undeserved, unexpected, all encompassing, infinite love, is that it takes great courage for us to accept it. It takes courage to say, "Lord, I am not worthy that you should enter under my roof, but only say the word and my soul shall be healed." That is our faith as Christians. That is what we are being called to believe. Jesus told the Centurion, "Let it be done for you as you have believed," and his servant was healed.

Where does God's love most need to abide in your life? If you could pick one thing, one place where you need God's grace to intercede, where would that be? What part of your life would you point to and say, "Lord, heal this." What is it that you would lay down before Him? If you could lay one thing down and say, "I'm tired, I'm tired of carrying this." We all have those things, those parts of our hearts that need healing. Those things that we use to victimize ourselves and separate ourselves from others. We are all one in our imperfections, we are all one in sin; that is what unites us, that is where we find common ground.

I grew up in Southern California, primarily Torrance, in Los Angeles County. My parents were divorced when I was 4 and my brother and my mom and I moved in with my grandparents. Our dad lived nearby and we saw him frequently, which was great, because divorce is hard. It's strange because you think that the kids won't remember, but they remember. I remember pulling out of our driveway in our station wagon with my mom, my brother and me, and my dad staying behind. I was 4. I used to think it was a dream, just a surreal memory, one of the glossy ones, but I remember, I remember the awkwardness.

My grandmother was very ill at the time and soon after we moved in she had to be moved to a nursing home. She had suffered more than a few strokes and needed constant care. After the divorce my mother had to work full-time and our grandfather became our caregiver. Two years later, when I was 6 years old, my grandmother passed away. I cried hysterically at her funeral. I did not want her to go. Later as an adult, I began to understand our relationship more because I was shown photo after photo of her holding me as an infant. I loved her red hair and I loved listening to the recordings of her beautiful singing voice before she was silenced by the many strokes.

Four years later, when I was 10 years old, my dad passed away unexpectedly. He was 43 years old. He died from complications arising from a temporary bowel blockage. His system became toxic and his organs failed and then he was gone. Dad died the day before Halloween and my mom wanted so much for us to enjoy the holiday. She thought my dad would really want us to enjoy it too, again, I was 10 and my brother was 13 and we lived in a great neighborhood for trick or treating. So she sent me to school the next day to try and enjoy the class party and the costume parade. But I didn't wear a costume. I knew everything had changed in my life, I knew my childhood was over. I no longer felt like the other kids, I was now on the outside looking in, wondering why the world did not come to a halt in light of my father's death.

I remember sitting in Mrs. Neri's 5th grade classroom at Edison Elementary School, my desk directly in front of Mrs. Neri's that day, writing a letter to my father in heaven while all the other kids were watching a film about whales. I was writing to him to tell him, "I know you are an angel now, and I'm just going to tape this letter to my upstairs window so you can come down from heaven and see it. I'm going to miss you so much. I love you, Daddy." I hid my letter inside a Halloween treat bag I had gotten at school that day. I didn't want anyone to know I was writing to my dad in heaven. I remember about a month later my mother found that Halloween treat bag amongst the clutter on the stairs going up to my bedroom. She read my private letter inside and mentioned it to me but I was embarrassed, so we didn't talk about it. After my father died, I just had a sense that I was on my own. My brother was a teenager, 13 years old and going through puberty and was now suddenly without a father. My mother was working full-time and grandpa was looking after us the best he could, but we were a handful.

A year later grandpa died and we were devastated again. I feared that our behavior made him sick, that because we were bad, misbehaving all the time when my mom was away working, that he died because of us. It was hard for me at 11 years old to understand what we were going through. In addition, to another great loss in our lives, we became latch key kids. I came home from school almost every day and was alone. Mom was working to support us; if she didn't work, we wouldn't eat, so after school and some evenings we had to take care of ourselves. I was alone a lot. My brother started high school soon after and he was wholly occupied and filled with teen angst.

I was truly blessed to have many friends with whom I would spend time with after school and would also be invited to spend the night over at their houses with them on the weekends. These friends and their parents were unexpected angels in my life, having me over for dinner, including me on family outings and two different families in particular always took me with them to church. When my dad died I wasn't angry that God had taken him because I knew he was in heaven and I just had this sense that I would see him again. I don't know how I knew or why I was so sure of it, I just knew. At the time, I even had vivid dreams about my dad, dreams where he would tell me he was not gone, that it was all just an illusion, that he had important work to do and had to fake his death. I knew he was still there, but our relationship had entirely changed and my faith in God seemed to actually deepen.

You know, when you experience loss like that as a child you grow up fast. Another year after my grandfather passed away, my uncle, who was also my god-father, passed away as well. It was just a series of unfortunate events.

Before long I was in high school and it seemed like a joke. I couldn't wait for it to be over. I had experienced such a dose of reality in such a short time that I started believing I could take care of myself. I didn't need anyone's help. My mom seldom had to ask me if I had any homework. Sometimes, I wished she would ask me more often because I knew other moms asked their kids that nagging question every day, but we couldn't afford the luxury of that kind of small talk in our lives. We didn't have the time. My mother did the best she could to raise us right. She often went into debt to give us things we wanted, just to try and make up for all that loss. I don't think that was the right thing to do, but she tried; what else could she do? I remember having moments of rage in high school, screaming at her for no reason because I was so angry at the world and needed someone to take it out on. She would try to discipline me for staying up late, sneaking out or ditching school but it was no use. I had been taking care of myself for too long and I was head strong. I blamed her for everything, I would tell her that I hated her, by saying, "What are you going to do? Really? I've been taking care of myself all this time!"

My brother and I threw everything back in her face whenever we were mad, as if she had control over any of our misery. It wasn't her fault. I was just angry, mad that I had been abandoned in so many ways. I didn't have the perspective to recognize that God was in those moments too, with us in our suffering. Looking back, I can see that everything my mom did was a prayer, a silent, thankless ministry. I don't think she recognized it herself. I think more so now she does. I have told her since, "Mom, I am so sorry, I remember being 16 and yelling at you, screaming at you about how much I hated you and how I didn't need your help, telling you to just leave me alone. I am so sorry!"

She said, "I don't remember that, I don't remember you being that way. You were a wonderful daughter."

I don't know how much she really "*doesn't remember.*"

I did learn how to take care of myself and truly as a result of everything we had already been through, I had set my mind on a goal of never letting anyone down or causing any unnecessary trouble. I got above average grades through high school despite writing all my own notes to get out of school and I actually became the kind of friend that other kids' parents always wanted their child to have.

During my junior year of high school, I decided to join the Army Reserves and that summer before my senior year, I went off to Army Basic Training. I had no idea what I wanted to do with my life and I figured the Army was one way to find out and would also give me money for college. I didn't know what I wanted to do. At one point I wanted to be a teacher but everybody wanted to be a teacher! If everybody wanted to be a teacher I didn't want to be a teacher. I was getting an "A" in auto shop; I could take apart a carburetor and put it back together again. I was the only girl in the class. So I signed up to be a diesel mechanic in the Army and I excelled in the structured life of the military. Needless to say, I had very few dates my senior year--perhaps throwing grenades during my summer vacation I was a little intimidating.

During my last year of high school, my mother was forced to file for bankruptcy and we moved into an apartment. After graduation, I worked two jobs and started saving for a car while living at home. My brother had already moved out. It was that summer that I became reacquainted with a boy I knew during high school who had since joined the military and was stationed nearby. He was handsome and charming and his parents still lived locally which brought him home a lot. He made me the center of his attention and that was very new for me-- and it felt amazing.

Finally, I thought, God had sent me the love I had had been longing for, pining away for, wishing on stars and praying for in my bedroom for years, waiting to be rescued from the loneliness and pain of everything we had lost growing up. I was finally getting the attention I had always wanted. I became lost in his presence, my better judgments gave way and just months before my 19th birthday I became pregnant. Someone had wrapped their arms tightly around me and for a while it felt like they would never let go. It felt right, at least until I realized I was in trouble. As soon as I found out that I was pregnant, I started negotiating with God to make it un-happen. How was I going to undo this? I was supposed to be the responsible one, I was that friend that everybody's daughter was so glad they had, and here I was pregnant, about to turn 19 and nobody knew how much trouble I was in. I told my best girlfriend at the time, but she didn't know what to do. All I remember her saying was, "Jenny, what are you going to do?"

"I don't know."

It was then I shifted into survival mode. It was then that I decided I didn't want anyone to know. I couldn't bear the look of fear on my friend's face. I didn't want to see it; I didn't want to admit that I needed help. "I got this, I'll figure it out."

At the time, I was working a second seasonal job as a retail cashier at a western wear store and when I went into work that day after taking my pregnancy test, another temp-worker, who I hardly knew, noticed something was wrong. Maybe because she was a stranger I was able to more easily tell her what was going on. She was a mother of two, however, the first thing she said to me was, "I know where you can go,

I know a place where you can go to take care of it." That would undo my problem.

I knew it was a baby. I knew what I was considering was wrong, but I refused to acknowledge it. I knew it was something people didn't talk about in polite conversation and I had a sense that it was something that would change me forever. Yet I was more ashamed of myself than concerned about the long term consequences. I felt like a failure, disappointed in myself for being so irresponsible, falling into the trap that made me a cliché. "This just in! A teenage girl from a broken home is knocked up."

I had no intention of telling my mother. We never talked about sex. My mom was very quiet about such things. In 5th grade, she signed my permission slip for Sex-Ed and that was that. I wanted my life to look like I had it all together. At that time, in those moments, I was filled with shame; the fear of being exposed overwhelmed me from seeing any other options. The truth was I didn't care what it would take to make it once again look like I had it all together. It seemed as though nothing worse could happen to me than people finding out how that I was stupid enough to end up pregnant after everything I had been through.

I remember, being pregnant and praying to God as I went through a McDonald's drive thru, "Lord, please tell me what to do. Just tell me what to do, Lord, so I don't have to make this decision?" I really wasn't praying though, I was bargaining. I already knew what I was going to do but I wanted affirmation that it was the right choice. Back then, I was negotiating so hard I thought God was on my side and wanted me to have an abortion. "Yes! The world is an awful place to raise a child. Yes! You had a terrible childhood, why would you want to be a mother? Why would you want to bring a child into this world?" I thought I could hear the answer, I thought I could hear God's voice, but really I had no answer. I had free will and perhaps if I hadn't been so scared of what other people thought, so prideful, or if I hadn't already made up my mind, I might I have heard God say, "Follow the heart I gave you, don't be afraid, I am with you." But I wasn't listening. There I was in a McDonald's drive thru having this dialogue with God before picking up my hamburger and fries at the window.

The day that I encountered the girl at work that told me where I could go to have an abortion, I went out into the mall on my break to use the payphone. I called my boyfriend at his barracks and I told him what I was going to do. I didn't ask him what we should do--I told him. I told him I was going to have an abortion. I didn't really give him a choice, and he didn't argue, I didn't give him time. Honestly, I don't know what he would have said if I had. He said very little most of the time anyhow. He was shipping out to Okinawa, Japan within a few days for a period of 6 months. Our relationship was going nowhere. He didn't even own a car. We were just a couple of dumb kids. I told him he would have to pay for half and I asked him not to tell his parents. I told him I didn't want anyone to know.

A week or so later, I lied and told my mom that I needed to borrow her car to attend a meeting at work. When I walked into the clinic's office, it was dark, as if everyone was more comfortable hiding in the shadows. The lobby had the kind of lighting that when you walk into the room, you immediately begin to strain your eyes and look for a light switch to turn the rest of the lights on because surely, it can't be intentionally that dark--but it was. The walls were dark wood paneling and were lined with chairs, more chairs than the space could comfortably accommodate or accept aesthetically. I went up to the counter and signed in but no one greeted me or looked up at me and I did not look at anyone else in the room, I just sat down. For all the years I would later spend working in law enforcement taking hundreds of suspect descriptions, I could not give you a single description of one person in that office, other than the doctor, which remains vague. I'm not sure if I ever looked up or made eye-contact with anyone. I knew what I was doing was wrong on multiple levels. It felt wrong and I could hardly bear it. I made another deal with God while I was sitting in that lobby, "Lord, if you just see me through this, I will never have children. If I turn this one away at heaven's door, I won't ask you for another chance at this, I realize this is my chance and I'm saying no. Keep this soul in heaven because I don't know what to do with it here."

A woman, perhaps a nurse, I have no recollection of her face, I honestly think I blocked it out, called me up to the counter to ask me some questions. She wanted to confirm if I had a ride home after the procedure. I told her, "No, I drove myself."

"Just a minute," and the woman stepped away for a moment.

When she returned she asked me, "Is there someone who can come pick you up?"

"No, I have to drive myself home. I don't have anyone who can pick me up."

"Well then, we won't be able to use anesthesia."

They took me back into an exam room and had me undress from the waist down and lie on a table. Then a doctor came into the room from a door near the end of the table. He didn't greet me, he just looked at them for a moment as if to say, "Why is she awake?" and then he got down to business.

No one said anything during the procedure to comfort me, it was as if, it was all they could do to make it seem as normal as possible but speaking to me, trying to make me feel at ease in that situation, was a bridge too far.

In that moment, everything was dark, I felt like I could not have picked a worse place to be on the whole planet. It was surreal. My sun was eclipsed and I knew I was at a point of no return. The pain was excruciating and it took everything I had not to pass out. It was unbearable. When it was over, everyone left the room. One nurse patted my arm before she exited, telling me it was over and I think she may have called me "dear." They left me alone to lie there, to recover. The table was hard and cold and I was racked with pain. I was 19 years old and I knew I had done the wrong thing. I knew I had made a mistake. And I knew that not only was my deceased father looking down upon me in disappointment but I knew I had also let down my Heavenly Father. I knew that it would forever change who I was. I knew I was no longer white as snow, the new me, the despicable me, had done something unspeakable. I had stained who God had created me to be. I tried to tell myself it was OK, but it wasn't okay. I had killed my baby.

I immediately started begging God to forgive me, as I lay there, but I couldn't hear Him, I no longer felt worthy of His attention. The only people who knew that I was there that day were my boyfriend, and my best girlfriend who had been with me when I took my pregnancy test, and of course, the woman who had helped me make the appointment. I hoped I would I never see her again.

My boyfriend wasn't able to go with me, but suddenly I wanted to see him. I went to his parents' apartment, looking for comfort but it was a mistake. He had no clue what I had been through. He was leaving the country for 6 months in just a few days and the only thing he was interested in was making out. I sat there on his parent's couch in utter disbelief. I never imagined someone could be so off their mark after what I had been through that day. The truth is, I was inconsolable. I just got up, hugged him goodbye and I left. He went to Japan and I didn't see him again for 6 months, to his credit he wrote me several letters from Japan, trying to stay in touch. Needless to say, it did not work out and we went our separate ways after he returned. And me, I just started burying it, shoving it all down, telling myself and others, the few rare folks I would open up to about it over the years, that it didn't matter. A month or two later, I was hired by the Hawthorne Police Dept. as a Police Services Officer, testing #1 out of 300. It was an incredible career opportunity and I dove into it, bought a car and moved out on my own.

Life moved on, later people would talk about being pro-choice or pro-life, and I'd say I was pro-choice. To my close friends, years later, I would say, "I don't have any regrets," telling myself it was all okay. I put on this tough exterior telling people that it didn't damage me, that it didn't hurt, and that it wasn't painful. I was trying to convince myself that I didn't make the wrong choice.

I never thought for one moment that I was denying God's love for me. I never thought that a baby could be God's love coming into the world for me, to fill all those empty places, replace all that loss. Instead of meeting His love with love, I created more loss.

I met my husband David, on the scene of a traffic collision I was investigating. He was a Battalion Chief for the Hawthorne Fire Department. Seven years later we were married and in 2002 we moved to Arizona. At age 30, after retiring from law enforcement to enjoy David's retirement, I suddenly wanted a child in the worst way. But David had had a vasectomy 15 years earlier while married to his late wife whom he had lost to cancer. So, I said either get a reverse vasectomy or buy me a dog. We went dog shopping.

David is what they call a cradle Catholic and I was baptized Lutheran and we both enjoyed going to church together. It wasn't long after we moved to Scottsdale that we found ourselves at St. Patrick Community on Sundays. Sitting in the pews each week, holding hands, and hearing songs like "His Grace is Enough" and "Jesus Messiah" would be played and I couldn't sing them because they would get caught in my throat and tears would fill my eyes and I would just squeeze Dave's hand harder. There was something about the words-- His love and that grace. I felt Christ moving in me, calling me forward to heal what I had tried to bury.

Unfortunately, my mom and I didn't have a close relationship. David and I also had moved away, which didn't help. I had always felt like there was a wall between us and then as I approached my mid 30's it started to occur to me that I might be the wall. I was the one who wouldn't go to my own mother and trust her with this most incredible female problem. I didn't give her the respect or the benefit of the doubt that she might understand or see a different outcome. I wouldn't let her help me.

After all these years, I finally decided it was time to confide in her, to come clean. I was 34 years old and had set my mind to telling her on my next trip home to Los Angeles for a visit. I committed myself to working on the pain; I committed myself to letting God in to heal what was broken in my heart.

I had always been spiritual, but I had never been a member of a church, a member of a community. I would go to church with different people at different times and I always knew God was there, and I knew about God's love. I knew that when I asked Him to forgive me that dark day, He forgave me, but I couldn't accept it. I couldn't accept that I was forgiven for a long time; it's not something that happens overnight in a broken heart. Forgiving ourselves for our shortcomings and failures is sometimes the hardest thing we ever do. Consider when you have simply said the wrong thing, or you spoke in anger to someone you care about and hurt their feelings. It is difficult to forget, let alone forgive yourself. How long do you carry that painful memory? How long do you go back and forth over it, replaying it again and again in your head? Regret without faith is a long term passenger.

I went home to LA for a weekend and as we were heading out to visit a friend, just the two of us, I literally heard God say to me, "You need to tell her today, on the way home." I was staring out the window watching the scenery flash by of the area where I grew up. My mom was driving and this was the first time during the entire visit we were alone together. Later that evening after our visit, while my mom was driving us home, 70 mph on the 405 Freeway through Carson, I told her. "Mom?" I started to cry, "I'm so sorry I've never told you this but when I was 19, I had an abortion."

Fifteen years later I finally had the courage to tell her the truth. She started to cry and I kept apologizing. "I'm so sorry Mom." Even then, I was still trying to diminish it, because I didn't want my mom to cry and I was ashamed, "It's okay Mom, you know I never really wanted children, I'm just so sorry I lied to you." I was still denying it to myself, trying to lessen the impact of the news on her and find relief from the weight of my own choices.

What happened next I never could have imagined. "I have something to tell you too."

I looked at my mom, who was still driving, trying to see the road through her tears, after I had just spilled my guts and we've barely begun to process what I just confessed, and said, "What?"

She began to tell me how 40 years earlier, before she met my dad, she had become pregnant in college and gave birth to a baby girl who she gave up for adoption.

My mom had planned to take the story and truth of her baby girl, my sister, to her grave, she said my brother and I would have discovered the truth upon her death as she keeps documentation in her safety deposit box. I had a sister. She went on to tell me that my father, my aunt and one of her close friends had known but she hadn't spoken about it in more than 30 years. I just looked at her, and I could see her pain. She had given birth to a child, made the hard choice to have the baby and give it up for adoption, trusting it to the world, to God, and she was deeply wounded by her choice. Her guilt was tremendous and now 40 years later, she was sharing all this with her daughter who had just told her she had an abortion. All the ways that my mother and I had struggled to have a relationship over the years, even as a child, suddenly made sense. She told me, "I always kept you at an arm's distance because you were such a painful reminder of the baby girl I gave away. I just had such a hard time with that, and I never thought I deserved to have a daughter as wonderful as you."

That evening my mom and I talked for hours. She went on to tell me that she had hid her pregnancy from everyone under A-Line dresses and coats through the summer of 1964. Then when she was 6 months pregnant, she was driving her "MG Midget" when a stake-bed truck hit her and literally cut the car in half and fractured her hip. My grandparents called the doctor to the house and when he examined her, he discovered that she was pregnant and together they told her parents. My mom said her parents supported her keeping the baby, but her boyfriend wanted to stay in college and was not interested in getting married, so they chose adoption.

The irony of our circumstances was overwhelming. A mother and daughter united in a strange cycle of suffering. I came home to Arizona, stunned. God had led me to tell my mom about my abortion, and begin to heal what was broken in me; a secret I had kept to myself for so long. Now after 34 years of life, I had a sister. God also wanted to heal what was broken in my mom. My mom didn't want to tell anyone, but I wanted to find her.

Within 6 months, I found my sister, Allison. She was married, living in California, and not so very far from my mother. Allison and her husband, Chris, have three wonderful children together. A few months after finding one another, we reunited our families and the day my mother met my sister was one of the most memorable days of my entire life. It was beautiful. Slowly and imperceptibly, grace was revealing itself to me; it was an awakening. He showed me how He could use my worst moment for His highest purpose. He showed me how much He loved me.

After coming home to Scottsdale, I sat in church in those same pews and when the music would play, again, I would cry. I didn't completely understand why. I knew but I didn't know.

I told my husband I wanted to become Catholic like him. I wanted to be part of a community that worshipped God and took care of each other. Yet at the same time, I was never going to tell anyone that I had an abortion. I entered into the year long Christian Initiation process at my church and every week we would in some way or another be asked to look at our lives and our desire for community, and answer, "Why here? Why now?" Early on, in the summer, during the "Inquiry" stage I was sitting with a few other candidates and two of the facilitating team members and we were talking about forgiveness. One of the team members quoted a movie about Saint Paul and said, "You know, it's not whether or not they are going to throw stones, it's how big the stones are going to be."

Suddenly in that moment, I got it. We are all broken, all fallen. In some ways we are all failures, losers, and wretches, because we all sin, we all fail. And we don't let ourselves off the hook, we don't let God's love in. At its center, sin is just a denial of God's love, a denial of our true selves. In all the ways that our lives are blessed, and in all the ways that we sometimes fall short, there is nothing we could do that would make God love us any less. I thought well, "Just throw 'em," I'm a broken mess; I am not worthy to loosen His sandals. There's nothing I can do to make up for what I have done. There are no good works that are going to get us into heaven, it is in our belief alone, our faith in God, that saves us.

I can wallow in my regret or I can wear my blessings well. I can be an outward sign of His grace and how it can touch one life, which could then touch others, and have the compassion to understand what that kind of pain really feels like. I am pro-every life. For me pro-life isn't so much about abortion as it is about clean water, clothing the naked and feeding the hungry. If I treat you with less dignity than I would treat the person next to you, then I've fallen short of God's call in my life and I would be a hypocrite, a fraud, a phony and definitely not a follower of Jesus Christ.

We are called in our baptism to love like Him, forgive like Him, be like Him. We are called to love every life, not just the babies and the unborn, but the seniors, the homeless, our neighbors and the poor in spirit. I think we are only here in this life to be love, to love one another as Jesus loves us. To follow Jesus, we must try and be like Him, to be His hands, His feet, His smile. I want Pro-life in my life to be more than a bumper sticker. Prayer is our way in.

Grace in Progress

············ *Prayers for the Beautifully Broken* ············

Help Me Follow

LORD,

Thank you for your peace. Thank you for being with me in every moment of my need. Forgive me for ignoring you. Forgive me for my petty anger when I disagree with your plan, your grace, at work in my life. Thank you for loving me anyway. Thank you for allowing me to fail and grow weak in this physical form so that I may become homesick for eternity with you. Thank you for making me aware of your presence, your love, in the smallest details of my day. In gratitude, I ask for your strength and your compassion to see where you are calling me to serve daily for your glory. Please give me your conviction and discipline to minister to others as you have ministered to me. Help me to recognize the people in my own life that I have judged harshly with disregard to your command to forgive them. Give me your heart, Lord, to see the needs of my brothers and sisters along the way. Give me the courage to humble myself to do whatever it takes to live the Gospel with my life. Help me to shine your love into every dark corner I find. Thank you, Lord, for asking me to follow you. Please help me follow you better.

Amen

Quiet My Mind

HEAVENLY FATHER,

Thank you for placing the desire in me to draw closer to you and be still. Thank you for showing me your love in the quiet moments of my day. Sometimes I spend my entire day running from one place to another; my attention and focus are far from you, until your gentle whisper calls me back from the edge. In those moments, help me once again remember that all these things I am chasing after are nothing in comparison to the Kingdom of Heaven. Often times, I am the creator of the noise, the drama and the endless to-do lists that I use to avoid you. Help me, Lord, to remember that I am more than worthy of your love and I need not run any longer. I now come to you and I ask you to please quiet my mind and open my heart. Help me to see myself as you see me, help me to love myself and others as you love me. Let me be a light to the world around me, a loving example of your abundant grace and mercy. Give me your peace, Lord, and make me holy.

Amen

In Trust of You

Dear Jesus,

Thank you for this day. Thank you for its ups and downs, its triumphs and its sorrows. Thank you for the opportunities today when I recognized that I need to trust you more. So many times today I fell short of living your call to love. Despite my life being overwhelmed with countless blessings, I chose many times today not to see your abundance and instead complained, lost my patience and took your love for granted. Help me, Father, to wear my blessings well despite the storms, the loss and my earthly grief. I want to trust you more and lean on my own ways less. I want to trust you so completely, that my worries fall to the wayside. I know that surrendering to your will, my expectations and my desire to control even in my pain will lead to your peace. Help me surrender. Please continually remind me, Lord, of who you want me to be, as I humbly profess once again, that I live to serve only you and your people. Please make me an instrument of your peace. Let all my thoughts and actions speak of only gratitude for your love and mercy.

Amen

Let Me Shine Forth

FATHER GOD,

I come before you with a bowed heart, humbled by your infinite love for me and in gratitude for this day. Overwhelm my spirit, Lord, as I come to you in praise and thanksgiving for your abundant mercy and thank you for the many blessings you have heaped at my feet. I want to love people with my life. Please help me radiate your joy and peace through everything I say and do so that all will know through my words and actions that I am your disciple. Let my life speak of your hope and salvation; let me be a legacy of your grace and love to others. Do not let me be lulled into the darkness of scarcity, but protect me from the worldly distractions that only serve to draw me away from you. Let me shine forth as your beloved, unashamed and sanctified by your grace. Let me never forget who you have called me in my baptism to be.

Amen

Stretch Me

LORD GOD,

You are calling me to great heights, raising me up to serve you in new ways that challenge and stretch my discipleship. I recognize my fear, Lord, and surrender it to you now as a sacrifice of my old self. I accept the gifts of your peace and mercy and rest in you with renewed confidence that you are transforming my heart in unprecedented ways. Help me to persevere despite all my doubts about the future and what seems like insurmountable obstacles of time and space. In you, Lord, all things are possible, let this be my new testimony to your people. Lead me in your ways, show me your paths and help me release my expectations and live more fearlessly in deeper relationship with you.

Amen

Glorify

CHRIST JESUS,

Teach me to glorify you in my every thought, word and action. Make me a miracle of your grace and mercy, a bearer of your word. When I allow darkness to invade, when I don't have patience in my heart for myself or others, remind me that I am your beloved, perfectly formed by you and called forth to shine. Help me to love like you and stand firm in my faith. Help me to always learn from my mistakes and continually renew my commitment to love others as I want to be loved. Let me see the Body of Christ through your eyes, Lord, without fear or prejudice, through a heart formed by a perfect love, forever glorifying your name.

Amen

Cast Out My Fear

HEAVENLY FATHER,

Give me your courage and your strength when I become weary and fear seeps into my heart. Help me to confidently live your gift of grace, and find gratitude even in the midst of despair. At this very moment, so many people are suffering in tragedy and illness around the world and I struggle to understand why this must be so. Let me not be dragged down into doubt when I do not see your plan, but lift up my heart into the mystery that every difficulty and loss may be used in serving the Body of Christ. I know people are being persecuted and exiled in your name. Help me, if only in spirit and prayer, to stand in solidarity with my brothers and sisters in Christ so I may help cast out their fears with the truth of your love, replacing their uncertainty with hope. Help me, Lord, to know and understand that as your beloved I am held to a greater standard by you; claimed as yours, I must be above giving into the worldly fears that plague my everyday existence. You are my Eternal Father, and you have called me to live, walk and share the gifts of your grace and mercy. Let me never forget this is my soul's vocation. Help me to be a light in the darkness that calls all your children home.

Amen

In My Grief

FATHER GOD,

The weight of my grief is greater than I can bear. Please fill me with the promise of your salvation so I may release this sadness into your hands and dance again in the glory of brighter days deeply blessed. Days that fed my soul and reminded me to whom my life belongs. Help me remember that you are my hope, the holy longing that sustains me in my hunger for one more day and chases the doubt back into the darkness. Bring me, Lord, into my searing pain so that I may recognize sorrow and choose to revel in the victory of your sacred joy and righteousness, unfettered by disease or loss. Give me your strength, Lord, to marvel in gratitude at the privilege of this life and this family and these friends you have sent to bless my path, however brief. Thank you, Lord, for those souls who have shown me your ways, shown me your face in their mercies and given me a sense of heaven on earth. I am forever changed. Help me to surrender my grief to your will and grow in compassion through the conversion of your love.

Amen

A Heart for Advent

LORD,

Help me to see you and only you in this advent season. Give my heart the strength to shine above the roar of the worldly rush. In the midst of my holiday routine, you call me to remember that you are the source of every good thing, every blessing, and every kindness. Help me to create a sacred space within my mind, body and soul that no amount of colored lights, or store-bought decorations could intrude upon. You are the light of the world and you call me to dispel the darkness in your name. My mind, body and spirit belong to you; use me for your purpose, Lord. You are my hope, my joy and my salvation. We wait for you now as we waited for you then. Bring us your peace.

Amen

Seeking You

LORD GOD,

Help me to remember that I am always in need of your mercy. Give me the courage to seek you first when my words and actions fail to glorify you. Help me to always hear your voice over my own negative inner dialogue. Create in me a fearless thirst for the peace you offer us in reconciliation. Break down the walls of my pride and doubt so that I may be transformed by your unconditional love and mercy. Let me never forget that I am forgiven, redeemed by your grace, transformed and made new. Help me, Lord, to live my redemption joyfully, filled first by your love, and ready to serve your people with a heart full of kindness and compassion for myself and others.

Amen.

Loving Like You

DEAR LORD,

I continually fail to forgive others and love like you. I am hopelessly imperfect and yet you still call my heart to perfection. You know my words and actions, my judgments and persecutions before they pass from my mind to my lips, sidestepping the gentle spirit you placed within me. Give me the courage to forgive others before I understand their offenses, as you have forgiven me time and time again. Thank you for the self-awareness and the confidence you have placed within me to learn from my mistakes and the free will to choose to turn the other cheek, and do as you have done. Help me to be steadfast in my walk with you. Help me to use the heart that you gave me to love like you, especially in the face of adversity. Sometimes the world makes me feel insignificant and small and I think one person's compassion couldn't possibly make a difference in the face of so much evil. Help me to stand firm in my faith, living like you, Jesus, with a sacrificial love for others that does not weigh the consequences of forgiveness but embraces the possibilities of them. Continually inspire me to renew my commitment to love others as I want to be loved.

Amen

Unfinished

Lord Jesus,

The race is not yet won, so please continue to prepare my heart for the journey ahead. As I strive for sainthood, as I stumble and fall over what I have done and what I have failed to do, help me to remember that I am an unfinished work in your hands. Strengthen me with your love and mercy. I recognize that I am incomplete until I submit to you. In this moment I surrender my past, present and future to your plan. Make of my life your masterpiece. Let your will be done and help me keep my eyes fixed on you, my victory.

Amen

Make Me
Dependent on You

Heavenly Father,

Make me dependant on you. Teach me to guard my thoughts and actions from any response that is not a reflection of your love and peace at work within me. When I am challenged, help me to set my ego aside and slow my reactions so I may better discern your will before I speak or act. Let your eternal love and validation ever flood my soul and release me from my false motivations. Make me one with you Lord. When I become lost, when I stray from you, help me, Lord, to turn around and see the servant's way. The raging storms that exist within my heart and mind are nothing compared to the shelter that is your constant strength and unceasing grace. Let nothing separate me from you.

Amen

Constant Companion

FATHER GOD,

Release me from my fear. You know me better than I know myself, there is no reason for me to be afraid. Help me to trust you with all of my being, so that my every doubt dissipates as my spirit falls into the safety of your embrace. Wherever I go, there you are with me. I never want to be without you. Thank you, Lord, for being my constant companion even when I did not seek you. You are my rock, my closest friend and confidant. Please bless me with obedience that I may always seek communion and counsel within you, the heart of my heart. Bless me with patience and enthusiasm as I await your return, confidently rejoicing in your holy mission at work in my life.

Amen

Help Me Listen

HEAVENLY FATHER,

Help me get quiet. Still the overwhelming internal rush of routine and achievement and help me settle into you and you alone. Help me listen. Let my searching cease and my anxiety fall away as I embrace silence to be in your presence. Teach me, Lord, to be expectant for you and let go of the need to fill every empty moment with chatter and the busyness of my own impatience. I am not what I do, but who you say that I am. Create in me, Lord, a grateful heart, satisfy my hunger and quench my thirst with your love and mercy. Clear the space within my heart of everything that is not of you and renew me again with the Holy Spirit. Make me a gift of your grace, an example of discipleship to others. Let the peace of your son Jesus Christ ever be my guide.

Amen

Broken

LORD,

Many times I have wandered so very far from you. Convinced I am not worthy of your love, I have forsaken you and the Holy Spirit you have given me to cover me through this life. I have made myself the center of attention and devalued myself through my words and actions, when I should have been drawing attention to you. Forgive me, Lord, for my selfishness and for doubting the legacy of love you have placed within me. I have sought comfort and looked the other way when it was easier than loving my neighbor. I have spoken harsh words and criticized others to promote myself above you. Instead of serving your people with patience, understanding and humility I have chosen my own importance. I now cast all these disparities of my sin and self-degradation at the foot of your cross, Father, and I ask you to use them for your good. I declare now, in this moment, that I am free of the sins that have bound my heart for so long and kept me from accepting my true inheritance in you. Thank you for claiming me as yours. Today, I am restored, resurrected and once again made whole through the power of your son, Jesus Christ.

Amen

In Fellowship

Dear Jesus,

Thank you for the gift of fellowship. Thank you for the incredible opportunity to experience the miracles of your grace and love through my friends and family. I long to be all that you are calling me to be, but I am immediately humbled by the fact that I cannot walk this path alone. At times I am so paralyzed by my fear and uncertainty that I turn away from the community that you have sent to minister to me. Please, Lord, help me see you in them. Do not let me disregard them when I most need them in my weakness. When I am lost in my own dark illusions, losing my connection with you, let them intercede on your behalf. Your presence within these hearts is an undeserving mercy, a sacred space of unconditional love. Please prompt me to ask for assistance when I need it and seek communion with your people whenever possible. Let my vulnerability be a language of love and affirmation to others so that they may also call upon me in their need. Our journeys are meant to be shared in companionship with you and one another. Give us courage, Lord, to open our hearts to one another and take our rest. Let us be relentless in seeking you through the loving hearts of your people.

Amen

Love Thy Self

LORD GOD,

Through your son Jesus Christ, you have given us freedom from sin yet we wallow in our lack of worth. Forgive us, Lord, for questioning your love for us and doubting your resolve to save us from ourselves. We must shift our focus from all the things that do not serve you and do not enforce the value of our souls. Help us to see your creation in us anew. Help us to let go of the worldly notions that we are not enough. Help us to release our old patterns of negative self-talk, self-sabotage and insensitivity to the intricate beauty that is our own unique human form. The form you gave us, the form you breathed life into and claimed as your own in our baptism and in your resurrection over the darkness of sin. Help us to resolve to listen only to your still loving voice within us as we gaze at ourselves through the many mirrors in our lives. Help us to hear your words instead of our own saying, *"You are a beautiful child of God. You are a child of the one true Father."* Lord, bring us your peace and let our anxieties and false expectations fall away. Let only your love and grace remain.

With grateful hearts we praise your holy name,

Amen

Loving God

LORD GOD,

Help us to be bold in loving you. When you call us forward, let us not be afraid to answer. Teach us to be still in your presence and allow your love to seep into every aspect of our lives. We want to have a more intimate relationship with you, Lord. Sometimes you call us to great works and we have no idea how we might accomplish them. We struggle and resist you at every turn because sometimes you are calling us to overturn everything that feels normal and safe. You are calling us to be extraordinary. Help us to be fearless in trusting you. Let us always remember that the obstacles we sometimes face are a blessing, an opportunity to recognize your presence and your will at work in our lives. Thank you for these opportunities for us to become better disciples. Let us be like the tide; the waves cannot roll or retreat without the pull of the moon. You are the moon, the stars, and the sun; you are all that is and ever will be, and the acceptance of your devotion to us is the ultimate goal of our love and obedience. Give us courage to clear away the obstacles to our faith that keep us from deepening our connection to you and only you, Lord. Help us to love you with our lives.

Amen

In Hope of You

JESUS,

Give us clarity to remember that we live in the continuous hope of you. We live in the beauty and the promise of our salvation in you. Give us strength daily to turn towards the light that is your love for us and help us resist our tendencies to rely on our own understandings, and desires. When our plans are interrupted by trouble or inconvenience, help us to remember that in those moments, when we are disappointed for not getting our own way, that You are at work. We submit that our will is not your will. Help us to see that you are calling us to stillness. Help us to re-center ourselves in the midst of every chaos and trust you above all else. Your love is our lighthouse and your word is our path home to you. Thank you for calling us to this sainthood, to this holy mission that is the daily ministry of our lives. We pray that we may always choose your love in our life over the emptiness that is anger, hate and regret. Let us be an example of justice and charity to one another. Help us live your love.

Amen

God's Prayer for You

DEAREST (*Your name*),

I love you so much. Nothing you could ever do would make me love you any less. I am so proud of you and the way you live out your faith and love for others with your life. I want you to trust me even more, I want you to give over to me every fear, especially your fears in trusting in the gifts I gave you. I need you to (insert your career/vocation/ministry), I need you to be my voice and a source of healing, forgiveness and renewal for others. So many others will come to know my love and mercy through your words and actions. Your (insert career/vocation/ministry) only serves to give me glory and free the hearts of the captive. Why would you hesitate to jump into the plan I have laid out for you? Your lack of faith and trust in me is not who you are called to be. There is nothing you cannot accomplish with me by your side. Trust that I have a plan for you and there is no place in this world that my hand cannot reach to protect, guide and love you. You are my beloved, you are mine, and I am yours forever.

Always,

Jesus

About the Author

Jennifer "JC" Beichner and her husband, David live and work in Scottsdale, Arizona. She was born and raised in the Los Angeles area and prior to moving to Arizona in 2002, she worked in law enforcement as a Police Services Officer and also served in the U.S. Army Reserves. Jennifer has dedicated her life to service, giving her talents over in ministry to women, seniors and teens as a volunteer high school youth minister on Core for Life Teen at St. Patrick Catholic Community Church in Scottsdale, Arizona. Jennifer also serves as a Board Member for the charity M.A.D. Girls Inc., sings in the choir and occasionally teaches "Prayer in Motion" classes. In addition to her volunteerism, and colorful background, Jennifer is going to school, working on two novels, edits for other writers and teaches group fitness classes at her local gym. In 2013, Jennifer was named "Woman of the Year" by the Phoenix Diocese Council of Catholic Women, an honor she firmly believes is a testament to how God works through our brokenness to reveal His love, mercy and grace to others.